ONE of a Kind

A GUIDED JOURNAL
TO CELEBRATE
ALL THAT YOU ARE

Written by Ruth Austin | Designed by Justine Edge

I wish I could show you...
the astonishing light of
your own being!

HAFIZ

You are someone worth celebrating. You. Just as you are.

You are someone who is full of love and hope and toughness and contradictions and dreams and wonders. You contain a whole universe of strengths and possibilities—all of them unique and all yours. It's time to see yourself as you really, wholly are and to recognize the ways that you are beautiful and worthy. It's time to see the magic you hold within. And it's time to let the world see it too.

Here is space to celebrate all that you are. These pages are a place to notice and record every good thing about yourself and your life, and they're a place you can return to for joyful reminders when you need them most.

Honor the journey that has led you here and look toward the paths you've yet to take. Believe in yourself. Live with intention and joy. Let your inner light shine brightly. There's nobody else quite like you.

Good friends are like mirrors:
they see you perfectly.

LAUREN MARTIN

These are all of the good and kind words I've heard my friends use to describe me:

...at the end of the day,
your feet should be dirty,
your hair messy and your
eyes sparkling.
SHANTI

Here are some of the things that make me laugh or bring happiness and light to my world:

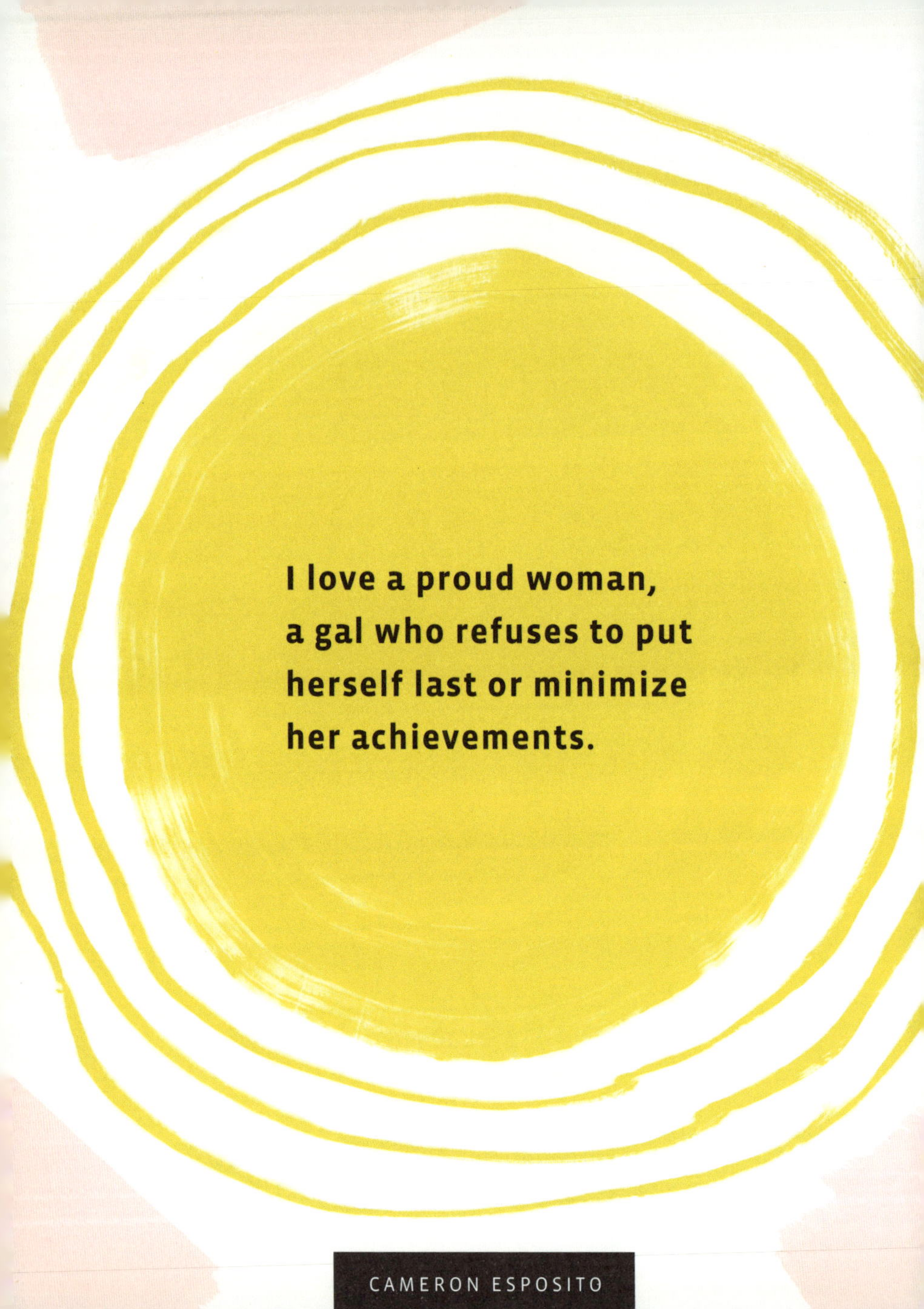
I love a proud woman,
a gal who refuses to put
herself last or minimize
her achievements.
CAMERON ESPOSITO

When I look at my life so far, this is what I'm proudest of:

We're all different,
all flawed, all beautiful.

ROBERT WEBB

Here is a list of small details I find beautiful about my appearance and my body:

...we are already found,
already truly, entirely,
wildly, messily, marvelously
who we were born to be.

ANNE LAMOTT

Here are some wild, messy, and marvelous parts of myself that I love:

What did you do as a child that made the hours pass like minutes?

CARL JUNG

When I was younger, these things and experiences filled me with joy:

There is no
duplicate of
you in the whole
wide world; there
never has been;
there never will be.

LOU AUSTIN

Life is a good teacher
and a good friend.
PEMA CHÖDRÖN

Life has encouraged me to grow in all sorts of unexpected ways. I wouldn't be who I am now if I hadn't learned these lessons:

Saying thank you creates love.

This is a list of all the things I want to thank myself for being or doing:

These beautiful days
must enrich all my life...
they saturate themselves
into every part of the
body and live always.

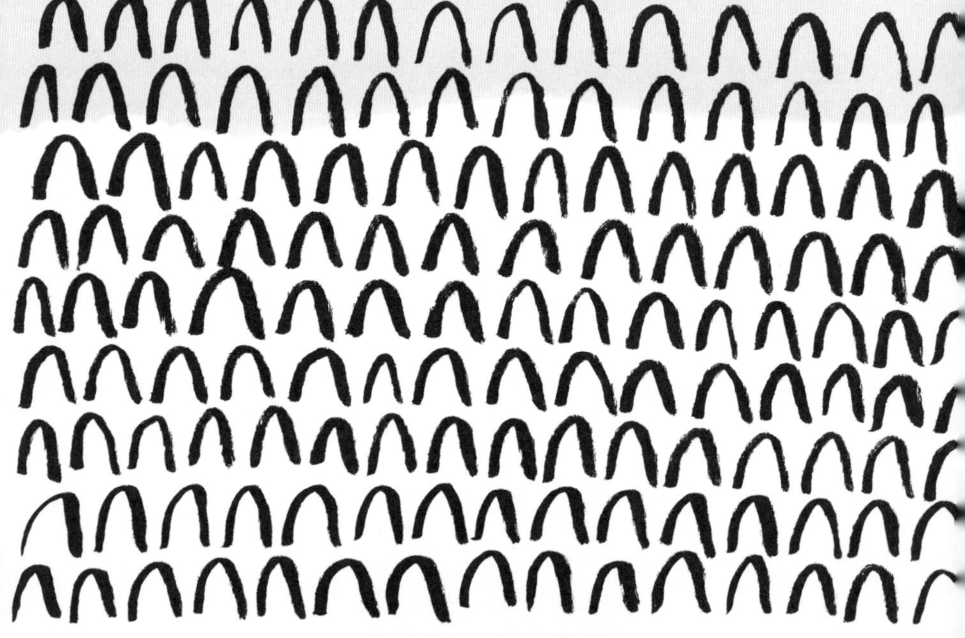

JOHN MUIR

If I could choose just one beautiful or fulfilling experience to always remember and carry with me, it would be this one:

If you could somehow postmark a letter back through time to your younger self, what age would you choose and what would the letter say?

This is something I wish I'd known when I was younger, or some loving words I wish I could have told myself then:

We are mosaics—pieces of light, love, history, stars glued together with magic and music and words.

ANITA KRIZZAN

When we choose "should,"
we're choosing to live our life
for someone or something
other than ourselves.

ELLE LUNA

I'll write down all my "shoulds" and "ought-tos" here and leave them behind so that I can choose what *I want* for me:

The most beautiful people we have known are those who have known defeat, known suffering, known struggle, known loss...

ELISABETH KÜBLER-ROSS

These are some of the challenges, hard times, and struggles I've known and overcome in my life:

There are days I drop words of comfort on myself like falling leaves and remember that it is enough to be taken care of by my self.

BRIAN ANDREAS

This is one thought that brings me comfort and happiness, something I can return to again and again whenever I need to cheer or restore myself:

I am a series of
small victories...
CHARLES BUKOWSKI

I will write down all my wins and victories here, however tiny, so I have a space to remember and celebrate them:

You have within you all wisdom, all power, all strength, all understanding.

EILEEN CADDY

"I love you" means that I accept you for the person that you are, and that I don't wish to change you into someone else... "I love you" means that I will love you and stand by you even through the worst of times. It means loving you when you're in a bad mood or too tired to do the things I want to do. It means loving you when you're down, not just when you're fun to be with. "I love you" means that I know your deepest secrets and do not judge you for them... that I love you enough not to let go.

ERIN MARIE MILLER

This is my space to say to myself, "I love you as you are," for any reason I want to, as often as I need to, until it starts to feel more natural:

Your body wants to live—that's all and everything it was born to do. Let it do that, in the safety you provide it.

CAITLIN MORAN

Here are some of the ways I care for, love, and look after my body:

Where you are
understood,
you are at home.
JOHN O'DONOHUE

These are all the people in my life who feel like home to me. The people who listen, and understand me, and accept me just as I am:

When you see beauty anywhere, it's a reflection of yourself.

SHAKTI GAWAIN

These are some of the beautiful things I'm seeing in the world right now:

If she got really quiet and listened, new parts of her wanted to speak.
SARK

I'm growing and changing every day. Here are some of the new things about myself that I'm noticing, new things about myself that I love:

You are a child of the universe, no less than the trees and the stars; you have a right to be here.

MAX EHRMANN

You live out the confusions until they become clear.

ANAÏS NIN

Right now, I'm working through the following confusions, questions, and uncertainties in my life:

...imagine yourself living in a space that contains only things that spark joy. Isn't this the lifestyle you dream of?

MARIE KONDO

I am grateful for these small and everyday objects. They're things I have chosen for my home, my room, or my life, or things that have meaning for me and reflect who I am:

Remember the compliments you receive. Forget the insults.

MARY SCHMICH

I give myself permission to write down every compliment I receive until this page is full of good words for me to read and enjoy:

Every day, you should have at least one exquisite moment.

SALLY KARIOTH

Here is one wonderful thing (big or small!) that happened today, or one moment where I felt truly and happily myself:

There is a voice inside of you
that whispers all day long,
"I feel that this is right for me,
I know that *this* is wrong."

SHEL SILVERSTEIN

Here are some things I'm happy that I've learned are wrong for me, things I'm comfortable saying no to:

Forgiveness. The ability to forgive oneself. Stop here for a few breaths and think about this… Again and again throughout the course of my life I will forgive myself.

ANN PATCHETT

This is a space to forgive myself. To discover compassion for my errors and mistakes, and know that I am still worthy of love. I will write down all the things I forgive myself for, and leave their weight behind me:

**Hello Traveler,
As you make your way along life's tumultuous highways, it's important to note that you should always carry a map, have plenty of fuel in the tank, and take frequent rest stops.**

OCTAVIA SPENCER

...the mind can only reflect the true image of the "self" when it is tranquil and wholly relaxed.

INDRA DEVI

Here are some ways I like to relax and unwind:

It's okay to do nothing
if you can once in a while.
It's okay to not be perfect,
to not get it all done...
take care of yourself.
Do what recharges you.

LEAH REMINI

I give myself permission to leave the following things undone, or to accept them as less than perfect:

...give to the world the
best that you have,
and the best will come
back to you.
MADELINE S. BRIDGES

No matter what might be happening in my world right now (challenging or positive), these are all the ways I am doing the best I can:

...live in the faith that the whole world is on your side, so long as you are true to the best that is in you.

CHRISTIAN D. LARSON

It is by love only that one keeps hold upon reality, that one recovers one's proper self...

HENRI-FRÉDÉRIC AMIEL

Here are some kind and loving thoughts about myself that I'm choosing to focus on:

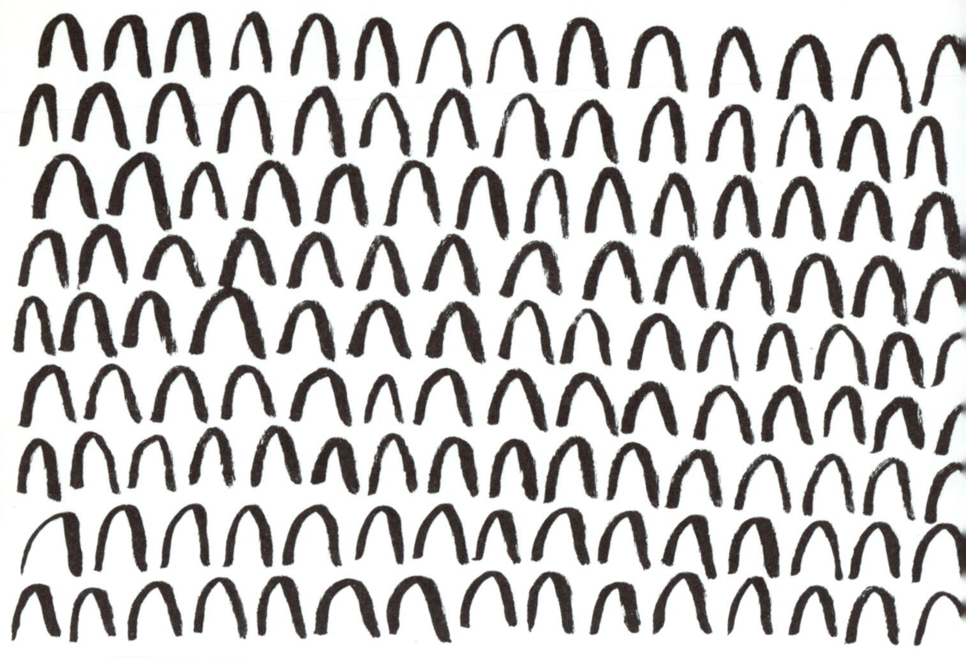

...character—the willingness
to accept responsibility for
one's own life—is the source
from which self-respect springs.

JOAN DIDION

I know that I am already accepting responsibility for my life and my happiness in the following ways:

We're complicated; we want to be so many things.

RASHIDA JONES

I will write down everything I am seeking, everything I want to become, no matter how contradictory it seems or unsure I am:

Work is love
made visible.
KAHLIL GIBRAN

Here are some things I work hard at, places where everyone can see love reflected in my life:

Love doesn't sit there like a stone, it has to be made, like bread; remade all the time, made new.

URSULA K. LE GUIN

You were made to be yourselves. You were made to enrich the world with a sound, a tone, a shadow.

HERMANN HESSE

Here are my talents and gifts. These are the things that make my heart sing and that I can offer the world:

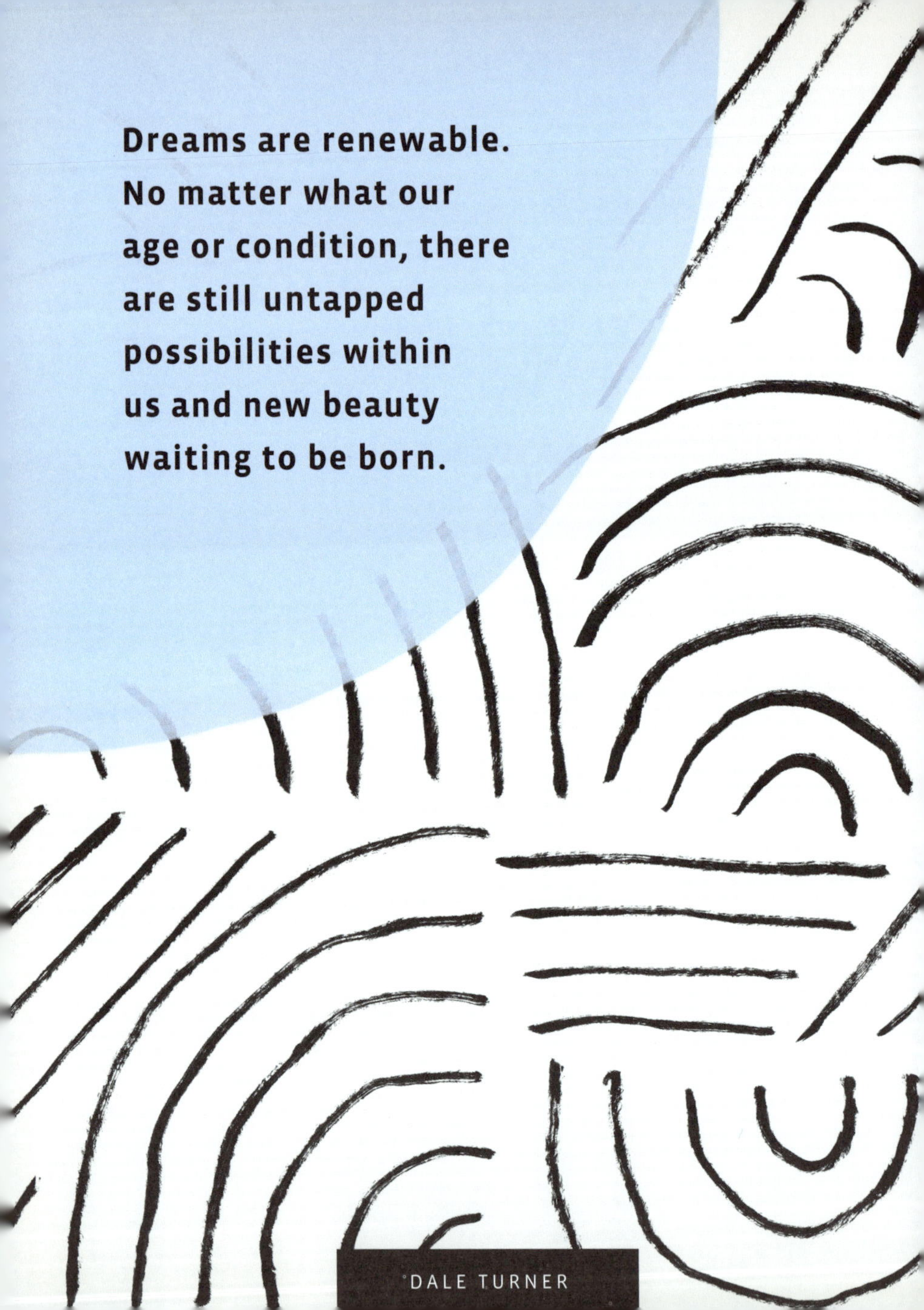

Dreams are renewable. No matter what our age or condition, there are still untapped possibilities within us and new beauty waiting to be born.

DALE TURNER

This is a list of goals that I want to set for myself and dreams that I'm dreaming right now:

...I take the pen and write:
I love you so much, my
heart is singing.

STEVIE SMITH

I will use this space to write a letter to my future self, describing all the things I love about being me, all the things that I offer, and all the ways that I am amazing:

If you could only sense how important you are to the lives of those you meet... there is something of yourself that you leave at every meeting with another person.

FRED ROGERS

These are some of the ways (little or big) that I can see I'm having a positive impact on the people around me:

This is my life.
Each hour is a
possibility…

AUDRE LORDE

Right now, these are the things I'm excited about, the things I can't wait to do, and the parts of myself I can't wait to share:

Unfold your
own myth...
RUMI

If the whole world could know just one thing about me, or hear just one amazing story that speaks to who I am, it would be this:

The privilege of a lifetime is being who you are.

JOSEPH CAMPBELL

For Sheila K., who celebrates with songs and champagne.

—R.A.

Written by: Ruth Austin

Designed by: Justine Edge

Edited by: Cindy Wetterlund

Library of Congress Control Number: 2019948016 | ISBN: 978-1-970147-08-7

1st printing. Printed in China with soy inks on FSC®-Mix certified paper.